AF271075

Exodus 3:14 (NIV)

God said to Moses "I AM WHO I AM. This is what you are to say to the Israelites. 'I AM has sent me to you.'"

To order additional copies of this book, contact:
BFBooks
Telephone: 1-203-710-1454
Website: www.bfbooks2016.wixsite.com/website
Email: bfbooks2016@gmail.com

8/5/18

I AM

"Love Yourself"

Written by Bridget Frankiln *BF*

Illustrated by Jordan Jones

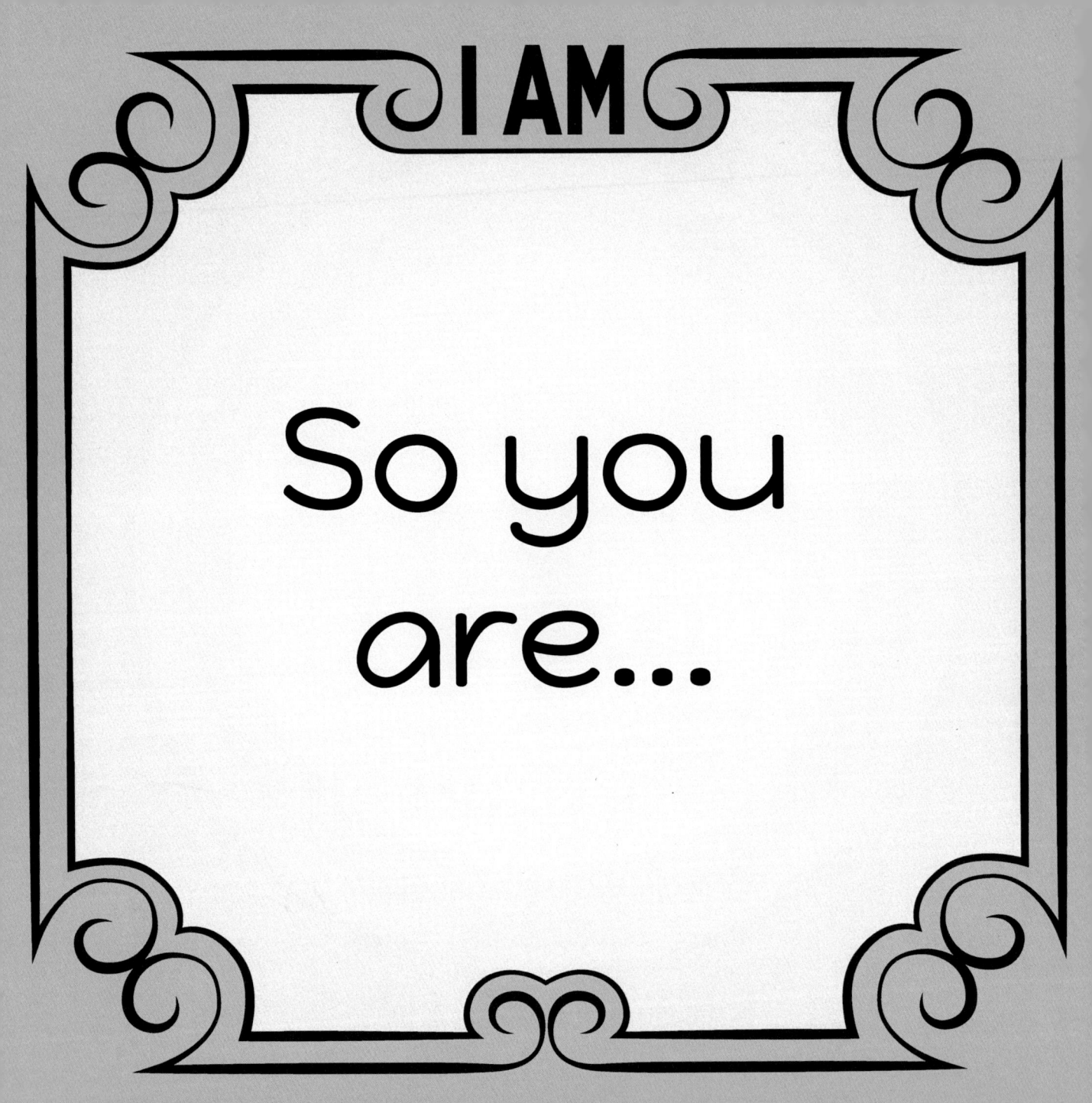

I AM

So you
are...

I AM

So you
are...

I AM

So you are...

Sons and daughters of royalty

I AM

So if anyone asks you who you are, tell them...

Exodus 3:14 (NIV)

God said to Moses "I AM WHO I AM. This is what you are to say to the Israelites. 'I AM has sent me to you.'"

Made in the USA
Lexington, KY
23 May 2018